Life in the
Crusher

Mysteries of the Deep Oceans

Trevor Day

Capstone
press

Mankato, Minnesota

Fact Finders is published by Capstone Press,
a Capstone Publishers company.
151 Good Counsel Drive, P.O. Box 669,
Mankato, Minnesota 56002.
www.capstonepress.com

First published 2008
Copyright © 2008 A & C Black Publishers Limited

Produced for A & C Black by

MONKEY
PUZZLE
MEDIA Ltd

Monkey Puzzle Media Ltd
The Rectory, Eyke, Woodbridge
Suffolk IP12 2QW, UK

Library of Congress Cataloging-in-Publication Data

Day, Trevor.
  Life in the crusher : mysteries of the deep oceans / by
Trevor Day.
    p. cm. -- (Fact finders. Extreme!)
  Includes bibliographical references and index.
  Summary: "Presents the science of Earth's deepest
oceans including the states of matter as solids, liquids,
and gases"--Provided by publisher.
  ISBN-13: 978-1-4296-3114-3 (hardcover)
  ISBN-10: 1-4296-3114-7 (hardcover)
  ISBN-13: 978-1-4296-3134-1 (softcover pbk.)
  ISBN-10: 1-4296-3134-1 (softcover pbk.)
  1. Oceanography--Juvenile literature. 2. Underwater
exploration--Juvenile literature. 3. Deep diving--Juvenile
literature. I. Title. II. Series.

GC21.5.D387 2009
551.46--dc22

2008024405

Editor: Cath Senker
Design: Mayer Media Ltd
Picture research: Lynda Lines
Series consultant: Jane Turner

This book is produced using paper that is made from
wood grown in managed, sustainable forests. It is natural,
renewable, and recyclable. The logging and manufacturing
processes conform to the environmental regulations of
the country of origin.

Printed in the United States of America

Picture acknowledgements
Alamy p. 18 (Photos 12); Corbis pp. 10 (Reuters),
11 (Jeffrey L Rotman), 15 (Chris McLaughlin); FLPA p. 6
(Frans Lanting); Getty Images pp. 4 (Tyler Stableford), 7
(Stephanie Rausser), 13 (Norbert Wu), 14 (Stephen Frink),
16 (Stephen Barnett), 17 (Zac Macaulay), 20 (Norbert
Wu), 21 (Norbert Wu), 23, 24 (Aldo Brando); iStockphoto
pp. 22–23; MPM Images p. 12 (Digital Vision); PA Photos
p. 25 bottom (Koji Sasahara/AP); Science Photo Library
pp. 8–9 (Carl Purcell), 19 (Alexis Rosenfeld); Still Pictures
pp. 1 (Jonathan Bird), 5 (Reinhard Dirscher/WaterFrame),
25 (Jonathan Bird); Topfoto.co.uk p. 8 left; Wikimedia
Commons pp. 26, 27, 28, 29 (National Undersea Research
Program).

The front cover shows a fangtooth, a deep-sea fish of the
eastern Pacific Ocean (Getty Images/ Norbert Wu).

Every effort has been made to contact copyright holders
of material reproduced in this book. Any omissions will be
rectified in subsequent printings if notice is given to the
publishers.

CONTENTS

Abbreviations **m** stands for meters • **ft** stands for feet • **in** stands for inches • **cm** stands for centimeters • **km** stands for kilometers

Dive in!

The **ocean** covers nearly three-quarters of the planet. Beneath its surface lies another world. Why would you want to go there? What would you discover? Dive in and find out.

As you duck your head below the surface of the water, your world changes. Unless you are wearing goggles, everything looks blurry. You feel the chill of the water. The weight of the water presses against you from all sides. The deeper you dive, the harder it presses. You have entered the world of the crusher.

Divers' secret words

If you dive into clear water far from land, the water all around looks the same color. Divers call it "the blue."

Plunging beneath the waves, you can dive down several feet. To go deeper, you need special equipment and training.

ocean the huge area of saltwater that covers 71 percent of the Earth

Deep!

In parts, the Pacific Ocean is about 36,000 ft (nearly 11,000 m) deep. That's 7 miles (11 km) from the surface to the bottom. Mount Everest, the highest mountain in the world, is 29,035 ft (8,850 m) high. If you could put it in the Pacific Ocean, it would be covered in water!

Coral reef growing under the water

Squeezed!

The water presses against the diver on all sides.

In the dim light, the diver uses a flashlight.

Water state

Water is magical stuff. It can change its form—or state—easily. Water often exists in different forms, side by side.

Penguins waddling on the **sea ice** in the Antarctic near the South Pole.

When water **freezes**, it becomes **solid** ice and does not change shape easily.

In the coldest parts of the world, water freezes at the sea surface. It forms sheets of ice called floes that can be several feet thick.

Water in **liquid** form is runny. The cleaner it is, the clearer it is.

freezes changes from liquid to solid   **state** the form of something: either solid, liquid, or gas

6

As the Sun's rays heat the sea surface, some of the water changes from liquid to **gas**—*water vapor*.

Most of the world's water in the oceans and seas is liquid. Imagine if you could level out all the Earth's surface—all the mountains, valleys, and the bottom of the sea. Then all the world's water would cover everything. It would be more than 1.6 miles (2.6 kilometers) deep!

Water **evaporates** into the air and becomes water vapor.

Three states

Water is the only substance on the Earth's surface that is often found as liquid, solid, and gas.

water vapor water in the form of gas

Killer icebergs!

Floating ice can spell danger for people.

*The iceberg that the RMS Titanic hit had **calved** the year before, in 1911.*

Imagine sleeping in your cabin on a ship. You are woken by a mighty crunch. Soon, the ship starts to tilt.

That's what happened in 1912, when the RMS *Titanic* hit an **iceberg** in the Atlantic Ocean. It sank into the icy waters, and more than 1,500 people died.

calved shed into the sea

Worldwide, 10,000–20,000 icebergs form each year.

Icebergs being calved into the sea from a **glacier** in Alaska.

Floating ice

Sea ice is frozen sea water. Icebergs are made of freshwater.

Icebergs are chunks of snow and ice that break off from glaciers on land.

More than three-quarters of an iceberg is hidden beneath the sea surface—which is why they can be hard to spot.

glacier a slow-moving river of snow and ice

9

The big squeeze

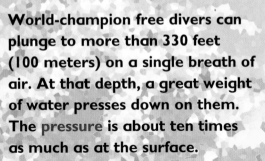

World-champion free divers can plunge to more than 330 feet (100 meters) on a single breath of air. At that depth, a great weight of water presses down on them. The **pressure** is about ten times as much as at the surface.

World-champion free diver Tanya Streeter, who once dived to 400 ft (122 m) underwater.

Most of a person's body is liquid—including the body's **cells** and blood. The skeleton is solid. Some spaces in the body—the lungs and ears—are filled with air, a mixture of gases. Solids and liquids are not squeezed much smaller under pressure. Gases, though, become squashed into a smaller space.

Bursting eardrums

Free divers train to deal with water pressure. They control the amount of air in their **middle ears** to prevent their eardrums from bursting.

cells tiny structures that make up the body of a plant or animal

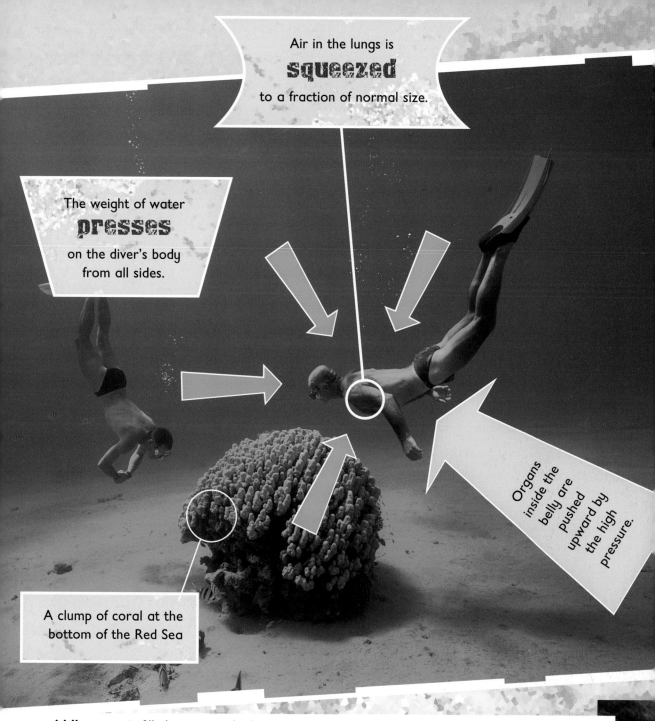

Air in the lungs is **squeezed** to a fraction of normal size.

The weight of water **presses** on the diver's body from all sides.

Organs inside the belly are pushed upward by the high pressure.

A clump of coral at the bottom of the Red Sea

middle ear air-filled space inside the ear   **pressure** the force pressing on an object's surface

Seeing with sound

Dolphins dive deeper than champion free divers. This takes them to inky depths where little sunlight reaches. How do dolphins find their way in the dark?

Good eyesight is not much help if the water is cloudy or the light is dim. Instead, dolphins "see" with sound by firing a beam of clicks and listening for echoes. This method, called **echolocation**, creates a "sound picture" that shows up rocks and other objects. Using echolocation, dolphins can find things as small as a pea. Dolphins mostly eat fish—which are much bigger than peas.

It's dark down there!

Sea water filters out sunlight. Less than one-sixth of the sunlight passing through the sea surface reaches 33 ft (10 m) down. By 330 ft (100 m) down, about one-hundredth of the sunlight remains. The lack of light in the deep ocean is one reason why echolocation is so useful.

Ah! Fish!

Speed of sound!

Sound travels about four times faster in water than in air. It goes farther too—sometimes thousands of miles.

Ping!

A dolphin fires a sound beam through its forehead.

Pong!

It picks up echoes through its lower jaw and directs them to its ears.

echolocation finding objects using sound

Under pressure

A lungful of air lasts a person a few minutes at most. How can a scuba diver breathe underwater for an hour or more?

A scuba diver takes a roomful of air down under the water, squeezed into a tank. Inside, the air is at more than 200 times normal pressure. A diver cannot breathe air at such high pressure—his or her lungs would explode! To prevent this, the **regulator** and mouthpiece deliver air at just the right pressure. People can dive down to more than 100 feet (30 meters) breathing this way.

Divers' secret words

Sometimes a regulator goes bad, and air rushes out. This is called a "freeflow."

scuba underwater breathing gear **regulator** equipment that controls the air a diver breathes

The bubbles get larger as they rise to the surface, and the water pressure on them becomes less.

The air breathed out makes bubbles.

Tank filled with air

Regulator and mouthpiece

The wet suit contains tiny air bubbles to give **insulation**, keeping the diver warm.

insulation layer that slows down the movement of heat

The bends

Ever tried shaking a bottle of soda and then unscrewing the top? The sudden release of pressure causes bubbles to burst out. Something similar happens when a scuba diver comes up too quickly after a deep dive. Dangerous bubbles of gas froth out of his or her blood.

During a dive, the diver breathes in gases, and they enter the blood. A trained diver learns to come back to the surface slowly after a deep dive. This way, the gases have plenty of time to escape. The diver slowly breathes them out.

*This diver is in a **decompression** chamber.*

Decompressed

Divers who come up too quickly go into a decompression chamber. The pressure inside is gradually lowered. This stops the divers from getting the **bends**.

As divers get nearer the surface, the bubbles grow as the crushing pressure lessens.

Bubble trouble!

If a diver comes up too quickly, tiny bubbles gather in the joints, especially the elbows, hips, and knees.

This painful condition is called

the bends

because the diver curls up, bending joints to relieve the ache.

decompression a drop in pressure

In deep and out of this world

Did you know that air can kill you? If you breathe air at the pressures found at 2,000 feet (600 meters) underwater, the air becomes poisonous. Scuba divers breathe a special mix of gases at this depth.

This scuba diver is wearing a full-face helmet for deep diving.

High-pitched

When scuba divers dive deep, they breathe a mixture that contains helium, the gas used in fairground balloons. It makes the diver's voice sound squeaky.

18

The diver's feet control propellers that make him "fly" underwater.

Is this man on the Moon? No, he's deep down in the ocean, wearing a hard-shelled suit. This way, he can breathe air at normal pressure while underwater.

The diver can move only at the joints.

This diver cannot use his arms and legs as normal.

His hands operate pincers in place of fingers.

The hard-shelled suit protects the diver from the high pressure outside in the water.

Monsters of the deep

If you came face to face with a deep-sea fish, you might think you had met a creature from outer space, or something from a nightmare. Thankfully, most deep-sea fish are no more than 12 inches (30 centimeters) long.

In the dark, deep ocean, many fish produce their own light. Some fish can switch it on and off. Fish may use the light to attract **prey** or to scare off **predators**. Many use light patterns to attract a mate.

Elephants on your head

At depths of 3,300 ft (about 1,000 m), the water pressure is 100 times that at the surface. That's the same as if six elephants stood on your head!

The fangtooth has hard, scaly skin, unlike most deep-sea fish. It sucks in fish and spears them with its long, sharp teeth.

prey animals that are eaten by other animals

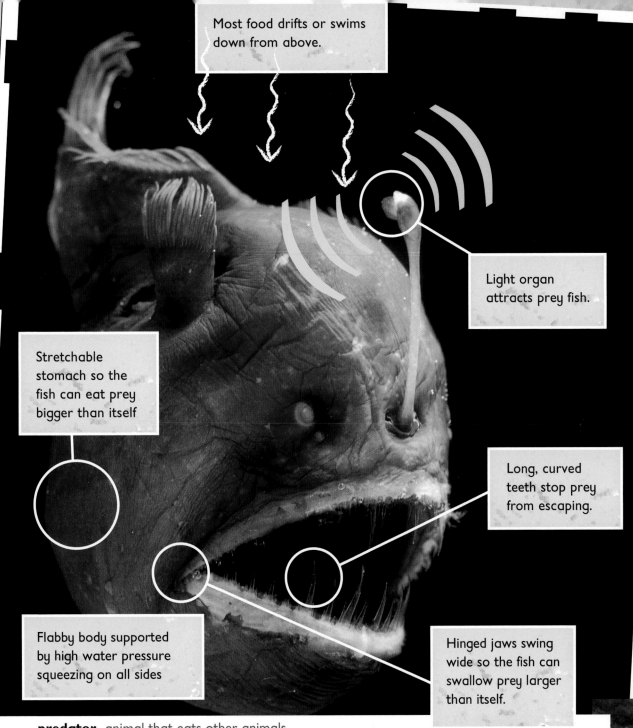

Most food drifts or swims down from above.

Light organ attracts prey fish.

Stretchable stomach so the fish can eat prey bigger than itself

Long, curved teeth stop prey from escaping.

Flabby body supported by high water pressure squeezing on all sides

Hinged jaws swing wide so the fish can swallow prey larger than itself.

predator animal that eats other animals

Dive! Dive! Dive!

An artist's view of a nuclear submarine launching a torpedo—a missile fired underwater at a ship.

Imagine not seeing or feeling the sun for months on end! Submarines can dive to depths of more than 1,650 feet (500 meters). Inside these giant "tin cans," sailors can live for months without coming to the surface.

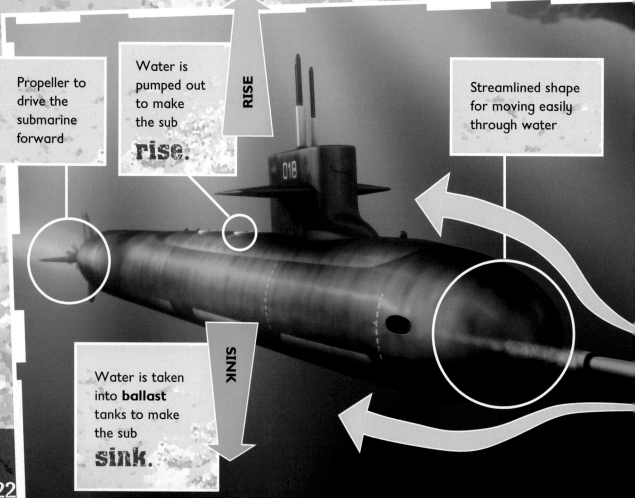

Propeller to drive the submarine forward

Water is pumped out to make the sub **rise.**

RISE

Streamlined shape for moving easily through water

SINK

Water is taken into **ballast** tanks to make the sub **sink.**

22

Submariners live in a world of artificial light.

Everything the crew needs has to be stored or recycled inside the submarine. Stale air, for example, is cleaned to remove the carbon dioxide that people breathe out. The air's oxygen is then topped off before air is pumped back into the submarine's living space. Phew!

Sailors' secret words

U.S. sailors call missiles "birds." A hatch (door opening) that trips you up is a "knee-knocker."

ballast weight added to make an underwater craft sink

Sounding off underwater

Some sea creatures use sound to keep in touch. Others use it to hunt. Some do both.

Herring live near the sea surface. During the day, they gulp air at the surface. At night, when they cannot see much, they "fart" to signal to each other. Their farts are high-pitched. Yet some whales, such as killer whales, can probably hear the farts. They hunt down the herring in the dark.

At night, herring "fart" air. It's a signal to other herring to gather in a tight shoal for safety.

blubber fatty layer under a whale or seal's skin

Sperm whales sometimes have giant scars on their skin from battles with squid.

Thick **blubber** keeps out the cold.

The sperm whale's blunt head focuses the sound beam.

Stunning

Some scientists think the sperm whale's sound beam is so powerful that it can stun its prey.

Imagine wrestling an animal with ten arms! Like dolphins, the sperm whale hunts using echolocation. It dives to 3,300 feet (1,000 meters) to tackle giant squid up to 50 feet (15 meters) long.

A 25-ft (7.6-m) long giant squid brought to the surface on a hook and line.

Diving deepest

In 1960, Don Walsh and Jacques Piccard dived to the deepest part of the world's ocean, the Mariana Trench. It is nearly 7 miles (about 11 kilometers) deep. The pressure is more than 1,000 times greater than at the surface. It's like having 60 elephants standing on your head!

When scientists explore the deepest parts of the ocean, they use **submersibles**—vehicles that have a spherical (ball-shaped) viewing chamber. A **sphere** has no corners as weak spots. It resists pressure well. The crew inside breathe air at normal pressure.

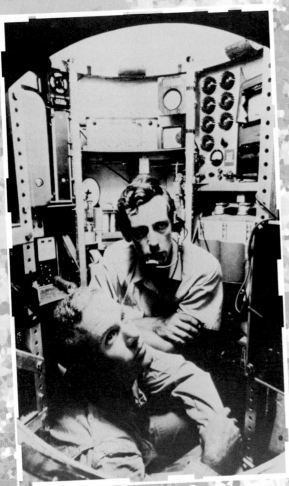

Walsh and Piccard, seen through the viewing window of Trieste, *which was made from Plexiglas—extremely tough plastic.*

sphere a ball shape

Walsh and Piccard dived in this underwater craft, Trieste. No one else has ever reached the bottom of the Mariana Trench.

FLOAT

This chamber contains gasoline. Gasoline is light and will help the craft float back to the surface.

About 9 tons (8 metric tons) of iron helped the craft sink. Walsh and Piccard dropped the iron when they wanted to float to the surface.

Viewing chamber. The viewing chamber wall is 5 in (12.7 cm) thick steel.

SINK

Lair of the giant worms

In 1977, U.S. scientists in the submersible *Alvin* were exploring the deep ocean at more than 8,200 feet (2,500 meters). Suddenly, looming out of the gloom, they saw an amazing sight. There were hundreds of 3-foot (1-meter) long worms, looking like giant tubes of lipstick.

Most of the deep ocean floor is chillingly cold, with little food and few large creatures. Yet in some places, **volcanically heated** water spews out from vents (openings) in the ocean floor. Thousands of giant worms, clams, and other creatures live around the vents. What do they eat?

The submersible Alvin underwater

volcanically heated heated by a volcano

Microbes float in the water and feed on chemicals in the vent water. The microbes, in turn, are eaten by other creatures.

Microbes also live inside giant worms. They feed on chemicals in the water, and make food for the worms.

*Giant worms living close to a **hot-water vent***

Hot stuff

Vent water can reach more than 662°F (350°C)—hot enough to melt glass.

microbes organisms so small you need a microscope to see them

Glossary

ballast weight added to make an underwater craft sink

bends a condition caused by gas bubbles forming in the blood when a scuba diver comes up too quickly

blubber fatty layer under a whale or seal's skin

calved shed into the sea

cells tiny structures that make up the body of a plant or animal

decompression a drop in pressure

echolocation finding objects using sound

evaporates changes slowly from a liquid to a gas

freezes changes from a liquid to a solid

gas matter that does not have a definite shape. It expands to fill the space of its container.

glacier a slow-moving river of snow and ice

hot-water vent an opening on the seabed. Water heated by a volcano comes out of it.

iceberg a floating ice block that has fallen into the sea from the land

insulation a layer that slows down the movement of heat

liquid matter that takes up the shape of its container but does not expand like a gas

matter the stuff that makes up all objects, whether solid, liquid, or gas

melting changing from a solid to a liquid

microbes organisms so small you need a microscope to see them

middle ear air-filled space inside the ear

ocean the huge area of saltwater that covers 71 percent of the Earth

organ a structure in the body, such as a lung, that carries out particular jobs in the body

predator animal that eats other animals

pressure the force pressing on an object's surface

prey animals that are eaten by other animals

regulator equipment that controls the air a diver breathes

scuba underwater breathing gear

sea ice ice that forms when sea water freezes

solid matter in a form that keeps its shape

sphere a ball shape

state (of matter) the form of something: either solid, liquid, or gas

submarine sausage-shaped underwater vehicle with a crew

submersible small deep-diving vehicle with a viewing chamber (cabin)

volcanically heated heated by a volcano

Further information

Books

Exploring the Oceans by Trevor Day (Four volumes; Oxford University Press, 2003)
A wide-ranging series that covers how oceans are formed, what lives in them, and how people explore oceans using technology.

Oceans Atlas by John Woodward (Dorling Kindersley, 2007)
Book plus interactive CD-ROM. Descend into the deep and follow giant sea creatures on their travels across the oceans.

Web sites

FactHound offers a safe, fun way to find Internet sites related to this book. All of the sites on FactHound have been researched by our staff. Visit *www.facthound.com* for age-appropriate sites. You may browse subjects by clicking on letters, or by clicking on pictures and words.
FactHound will fetch the best sites for you!

Films

Deep Blue directed by www.bbc.co.uk/films/ Alastair Fothergill, Andy Byatt and Martha Holmes (BBC, 2004)
Amazing underwater sequences from the team that made the Blue Planet TV series. Parental guidance required.

Secrets of the Titanic directed by Robert D. Ballard and Nicolas Noxon (National Geographic/Warner, 1986)
Underwater vehicles discover the wreck of the RMS *Titanic*.

Index